ANNA QUINDLEN
HOW READING CHANGED MY LIFE

"In books I have traveled, not only to other worlds, but into my own. I learned who I was and who I wanted to be, what I might aspire to, and what I might dare to dream about my world and myself. More powerfully and persuasively than from the 'shalt nots' of the Ten Commandments. I learned the difference between good and evil, right and wrong. One of my favorite childhood books, *A Wrinkle in Time,* described that evil, that wrong, existing in a different dimension from our own. But I felt that I, too, existed much of the time in a different dimension from everyone else I knew. There was waking, and there was sleeping. And then there were books, a kind of parallel universe in which anything might happen and frequently did, a universe in which I might be a newcomer but was never really a stranger. My real, true world. My perfect island."

Also by Anna Quindlen

Black and Blue
One True Thing
Thinking Out Loud
Object Lessons
Living Out Loud
A Short Guide to a Happy Life
Blessings
Loud and Clear
Being Perfect
Rise and Shine
Good Dog. Stay.

BOOKS FOR CHILDREN
The Tree That Came to Stay
Happily Ever After

HOW
READING
CHANGED
MY LIFE

ANNA QUINDLEN

BALLANTINE BOOKS • NEW YORK

A Ballantine Books Trade Paperback Edition

Published in the United States by Ballantine Books, an imprint of
The Random House Publishing Group, a division of Random House, Inc.,
New York, and simultaneously in Canada by Random House of Canada
Limited, Toronto.

Grateful acknowledgment is made to the following for permission to reprint
previously published material:

Christopher Franceschelli for permission to reprint an excerpt from
his Letter to the Editor of *The Horn Book,* August/September 1997. Used by
permission of the author.

Katherine Paterson for permission to reprint excerpts from her lecture given
at the New York Public Library in 1997. Copyright © 1997 by Katherine
Paterson. Used by permission of the author.

www.ballantinebooks.com

Library of Congress Cataloging-in-Publication Data
Quindlen, Anna.
How reading changed my life / Anna Quindlen.—1st ed.
p.   cm — (The library of contemporary thought)
ISBN 978-0-345-42278-1 (alk. paper)
1. Quindlen, Anna—Books and reading.   2. Women authors, American—
20th century—Biography.   3. Books and reading—
United States—History—20th century.   I. Title.   II. Series: Library
of contemporary thought (Ballantine Publishing Group)
PS3567.U336Z468   1998
813'.54—dc21
[B]   98-30191
CIP

Text design by Holly Johnson
Cover design and art by Ruth Ross

Printed in the United States of America

First Edition: August 1998

16   18   19   17

Books, books, books!
I had found the secret of a garret-room
Piled high with cases in my father's name,
Piled high, packed large,—where, creeping in
    and out
Among the giant fossils of my past,
Like some small nimble mouse between
    the ribs
Of a mastodon, I nibbled here and there
At this or that box, pulling through the gap,
In heats of terror, haste, victorious joy,
The first book first. And how I felt it beat
Under my pillow, in the morning's dark,
An hour before the sun would let me read!
My books!

        —ELIZABETH BARRETT BROWNING,

              AURORA LEIGH

How many a man has dated a new era in his life from the reading of a book. The book exists for us perchance which will explain our miracles and reveal new ones.

      —HENRY DAVID THOREAU

THE STORIES ABOUT my childhood, the ones that stuck, that got told and retold at dinner tables, to dates as I sat by red-faced, to my own children by my father later on, are stories of running away. Some are stories of events I can't remember, that I see and feel only in the retelling: the toddler who wandered down the street while her mother was occupied with yet another baby and was driven home by the police; the little girl who was seen by a neighbor ambling down the alley a block north of her family's home; the child who appeared on her grandparents' doorstep and wasn't quite sure whether anyone knew she'd come so far on her own.

Other times I remember myself. I remember taking the elevated train to downtown Philadelphia because, like Everest, it was there, a spired urban Oz so other from the quiet flat streets of the suburbs where we lived. I remember riding my bicycle for miles to the neighborhood where my aunt and uncle lived, a narrow avenue of brick row houses with long boxcar backyards. I remember going to the airport with my parents when I was thirteen and reading the destinations board, seeing all the places I could go: San Juan, Cincinnati, Los Angeles, London. I remember loving motels; the cheap heavy silverware on airplanes; the smell of plastic, disinfectant, and mildew on the old Greyhound buses. I remember watching trains click by, a blur of grey and the diamond glitter of sunshine on glass, and wishing I was aboard.

The odd thing about all this is that I had a lovely childhood in a lovely place. This is the way I remember it; this is the way it was. The neighborhood where I grew up was the sort of place in which people dream of raising children—pretty, privileged but not rich, a small but satisfying spread of center-hall colonials, old roses, rhododendrons, and quiet roads. We walked to school, wandered wild in the summer, knew everyone and all their brothers and sisters, too. Some of the people I went to school with, who I sat next to in sixth and seventh grade, still live there, one or two in the houses that their parents once owned.

Not long ago, when I was in town on business, I determined to test my memories against the reality and drove to my old block, my old school, the homes of my closest friends, sure that I had inflated it all in my mind. But the houses were no smaller, the flowers no less bright. It was as fine as I had remembered—maybe more so, now when so much of the rest of the world has come to seem dingy and diminished.

Yet there was always in me, even when I was very small, the sense that I ought to be somewhere else. And wander I did, although, in my everyday life, I had nowhere to go and no imaginable reason on earth why I should want to leave. The buses took to the interstate without me; the trains sped by. So I wandered the world through books. I went to Victorian England in the pages of *Middlemarch* and *A Little Princess*, and to Saint Petersburg before the fall of the tsar with *Anna Karenina*. I went to Tara, and Manderley, and Thornfield Hall, all those great houses, with their high ceilings and high drama, as I read *Gone with the Wind*, *Rebecca*, and *Jane Eyre*.

When I was in eighth grade I took a scholarship test for a convent school, and the essay question began with a quotation: "It is a far, far better thing that I do, than I have ever done; it is a far, far better rest that I go to, than I have ever known." Later, over a stiff and awkward lunch of tuna-fish salad, some of the other girls at my table were perplexed by the source of the quotation and what it meant, and I was certain, at that moment, weeks before my parents got the letter from the nuns, that the scholarship was mine. How many times had I gone up the steps to the guillotine with Sydney Carton as he went to that far, far better rest at the end of *A Tale of Two Cities*?

Like so many of the other books I read, it never seemed to me like a book, but like a place I had lived in, had visited and would visit again, just as all the people in them, every blessed one—Anne of Green Gables, Heidi, Jay Gatsby, Elizabeth Bennet, Scarlett O'Hara, Dill and Scout, Miss Marple, and Hercule Poirot—were more real than the real people I knew. My home was in that pleasant place outside Philadelphia, but I really lived somewhere else. I lived within the covers of books and those books were more real to me than any other thing in my life. One poem committed to memory in grade school survives in my mind. It is by Emily Dickinson: "There is no Frigate like a Book / To take us Lands away / Nor any coursers like a Page / Of prancing Poetry."

Perhaps only a truly discontented child can become as seduced by books as I was. Perhaps restlessness is a necessary corollary of devoted literacy. There was a club chair in our house, a big one, with curled arms and a square ottoman; it sat in one corner of the living room, catty-corner to the fireplace, with a barrel table next to it. In my mind I am always sprawled in it, reading with my skinny, scabby legs slung over one of its arms. "It's a beautiful day," my mother is saying; she said that always, often, autumn, spring, even when there was a fresh snowfall. "All your friends are outside." It was true; they always were. Sometimes I went out with them, coaxed into the street, out into the fields, down by the creek, by the lure of what I knew intuitively was normal childhood, by the promise of being what I knew instinctively was a normal child, one who lived, raucous, in the world.

I have clear memories of that sort of life, of lifting the rocks in the creek that trickled through Naylor's Run to search for crayfish, of laying pennies on the tracks of the trolley and running to fetch them, flattened, when the trolley had passed. But at base it was never any good. The best part of me was always at home, within some book that had been laid flat on the table to mark my place, its imaginary people waiting for me to return and bring them to life. That was where the real people were, the trees that moved in the wind, the still, dark waters. I won a bookmark in a spelling bee during that time with these words of Montaigne upon it in gold: "When I am reading a book, whether wise or silly, it seems to me to be alive and talking to me." I found that bookmark not long ago, at the bottom of a box, when my father was moving.

In the years since those days in that club chair I have learned that I was not alone in this, although at the time I surely was, the only child I knew, or my parents knew, or my friends knew, who preferred reading to playing kick-the-can or ice-skating or just sitting on the curb breaking sticks and scuffing up dirt with a sneaker in summer. In books I have traveled, not only to other worlds, but into my own. I learned who I was and who I wanted to be, what I might aspire to, and what I might dare to dream about my world and myself. More powerfully and persuasively than from the "shalt nots" of the Ten Commandments, I learned the difference between good and evil, right and wrong. One of my favorite childhood books, *A Wrinkle in Time,* described that evil, that wrong, existing in a different dimension from our own. But I felt that I, too, existed much of the time in a different dimension from everyone else I knew. There was waking, and there was sleeping. And then there were books, a kind of parallel universe in which anything might happen and frequently did, a universe in which I might be a newcomer but was never really a stranger. My real, true world. My perfect island.

Years later I would come to discover, as Robinson Crusoe did when he found Man Friday, that I was not alone in that world or on that island. I would discover (through reading, naturally) that while I was sprawled, legs akimbo, in that chair with a book, Jamaica Kincaid was sitting in the glare of the Caribbean sun in Antigua reading in that same way that I did, as though she was starving and the book was bread. When she was grown-up, writing books herself, winning awards for her work, she talked in one of her memoirs of ignoring her little brother when she was supposed to be looking after him: "I liked reading a book much more than I liked looking after him (and even now I like reading a book more than I like looking after my own children . . .)."

While I was in that club chair with a book, Hazel Rochman and her husband were in South Africa, burying an old tin trunk heavy with hardcovers in the backyard, because the police might raid their house and search it for banned books. Rochman, who left Johannesburg for Chicago and became an editor for the American Library Association's *Booklist*, summed up the lessons learned from that night, about the power of reading, in a way I would have recognized even as a girl. "Reading makes immigrants of us all," she wrote years later. "It takes us away from home, but, most important, it finds homes for us everywhere."

While I was in that club chair with a book,

Oprah Winfrey was dividing her childhood between her mother in Milwaukee and her father in Nashville, but finding her most consistent home between the covers of her books. Even decades later, when she had become the host of her eponymous talk show, one of the world's highest-paid entertainers, and the founder of an on-air book club that resulted in the sale of millions of copies of serious literary novels, Winfrey still felt the sting as she talked to a reporter from *Life* magazine: "I remember being in the back hallway when I was about nine—I'm going to try to say this without crying—and my mother threw the door open and grabbed a book out of my hand and said, 'You're nothing but a something-something bookworm. Get your butt outside! You think you're better than the other kids.' I was treated as though something was wrong with me because I wanted to read all the time."

Reading has always been my home, my sustenance, my great invincible companion. "Book love," Trollope called it. "It will make your hours pleasant to you as long as you live." Yet of all the many things in which we recognize some universal comfort— God, sex, food, family, friends—reading seems to be the one in which the comfort is most undersung, at least publicly, although it was really all I thought of, or felt, when I was eating up book after book, running away from home while sitting in that chair, traveling around the world and yet never leaving the room. I did not read from a sense of superiority, or advancement, or even learning. I read because I loved it more than any other activity on earth.

By the time I became an adult, I realized that while my satisfaction in the sheer act of reading had not abated in the least, the world was often as hostile, or at least as blind, to that joy as had been my girlfriends banging on our screen door, begging me to put down the book—"that stupid book," they usually called it, no matter what book it happened to be. While we pay lip service to the virtues of reading, the truth is that there is still in our culture something that suspects those who read too much, whatever reading too much means, of being lazy, aimless dreamers, people who need to grow up and come outside to where real life is, who think themselves superior in their separateness.

There is something in the American character that is even secretly hostile to the act of aimless reading, a certain hale and heartiness that is suspicious of reading as anything more than a tool for advancement. This is a country that likes confidence but despises hubris, that associates the "nose in the book" with the same sense of covert superiority that Ms. Winfrey's mother did. America is also a nation that prizes sociability and community, that accepts a kind of psychological domino effect: alone leads to loner, loner to loser. Any sort of turning away from human contact is suspect, especially one that interferes with the go-out-and-get-going ethos that seems to be at the heart of our national character. The image of American presidents that stick are those that portray them as men of action: Theodore Roosevelt on safari, John Kennedy throwing a football around with his brothers. There is only Lincoln as solace to the inveterate reader, a solitary figure sitting by the fire, saying, "My best friend is a person who will give me a book I have not read."

There also arose, as I was growing up, a kind of careerism in the United States that sanctioned reading only if there was some point to it. Students at the nation's best liberal arts colleges who majored in philosophy or English were constantly asked what they were "going to do with it," as though intellectual pursuits for their own sake had had their day, and lost it in the press of business. Reading for pleasure was replaced by reading for purpose, and a kind of dogged self-improvement: whereas an executive might learn far more from *Moby Dick* or *The Man in the Grey Flannel Suit*, the book he was expected to have read might be *The Seven Habits of Highly Successful People*. Reading for pleasure, spurred on by some interior compulsion, became as suspect as getting on the subway to

ride aimlessly from place to place, or driving from nowhere to nowhere in a car. I like to do both those
things, too, but not half so much as reading.

For many years I worked in the newspaper business, where every day the production of the product
stands as a flimsy but eloquent testimony to the thirst
for words, information, experience. But, for working
journalists, reading in the latter half of the twentieth
century was most often couched as a series of problems to be addressed in print: were children in public
schools reading poorly? Were all Americans reading
less? Was the printed word giving way to the spoken
one? Had television and the movies supplanted
books? The journalistic answer, most often, was yes,
yes, yes, yes, buttressed by a variety of statistics that,
as so often happens, were massaged to prove the
point: reading had fallen upon hard times. And in
circles devoted to literary criticism, among the pro-
fessors of literature, the editors and authors of fiction,
there was sometimes a kind of horrible exclusivity surrounding discussions of reading. There was good reading, and there was bad reading. There was the worthy,
and the trivial. This was always couched in terms of
taste, but it tasted, smelled, and felt unmistakably like
snobbery.

None of this was new, except, in its discovering,
to me. Reading has always been used as a way to divide
a country and a culture into the literati and everyone

else, the intellectually worthy and the hoi polloi. But in the fifteenth century Gutenberg invented the printing press, and so began the process of turning the book from a work of art for the few into a source of information for the many. After that, it became more difficult for one small group of people to lay an exclusive claim to books, to seize and hold reading as their own. But it was not impossible, and it continued to be done by critics and scholars. When I began to read their work, in college, I was disheartened to discover that many of them felt that the quality of poetry and prose, novels and history and biography, was plummeting into some intellectual bargain basement. But reading saved me from despair, as it always had, for the more I read the more I realized it had always been thus, and that apparently an essential part of studying literature, whether in 1840, 1930, or 1975, was to conclude that there had once been a golden age, and it was gone. "The movies consume so large a part of the leisure of the country that little time is left for other things," the trade magazine of the industry, *Publishers Weekly*, lamented in 1923. "The novel can't compete with cars, the movies, television, and liquor," the French writer Louis-Ferdinand Céline said in 1960.

There was certainly no talk of comfort and joy, of the lively subculture of those of us who forever fell asleep with a book open on our bedside tables, whether bought or borrowed. Of those of us who comprise the real clan of the book, who read not to judge the reading of others but to take the measure of ourselves. Of those of us who read because we love it more than anything, who feel about bookstores the way some people feel about jewelers. The silence about this was odd, both because there are so many of us and because we are what the world of books is really about. We are the people who once waited for the newest installment of Dickens's latest novel and who kept battered copies of *Catcher in the Rye* in our back pockets and our backpacks. We are the ones who saw to it that *Pride and Prejudice* never went out of print.

But there was little public talk of us, except in memoirs like Ms. Kincaid's. Nothing had changed since I was a solitary child being given embossed leather bookmarks by relatives for Christmas. It was still in the equivalent of the club chairs that we found one another: at the counters in bookstores with our arms full, at the front desks in libraries, at school, where teachers introduced us to one another—and, of course, in books, where book-lovers make up a lively subculture of characters. "Until I feared I would lose it, I never loved to read. One does not love breathing," says Scout in *To Kill a Mockingbird*.

Reading is like so much else in our culture, in all cultures: the truth of it is found in its people and not in its pundits and its professionals. If I believed what I read about reading I would despair. But instead there are letters from readers to attend to, like the one from a girl who had been given one of my books by her mother and began her letter, "I guess I am what some people would call a bookworm."

"So am I," I wrote back.

Books are to be called for and supplied on the assumption that the process of reading is not a half-sleep; but in the highest sense an exercise, a gymnastic struggle; that the reader is to do something for himself.

—WALT WHITMAN

IT STILL SEEMS infinitely mysterious to me that there are some of us who have built not a life but a self, based largely on our hunger for what are a series of scratches on a piece of paper. There remain in the world, six millennia after a list of livestock on a clay tablet created reading, cultures in which the written word is a mystery, a luxury, even a redundancy. Stories are still told beside fires and streams by people bent almost double from working in the fields, told as richly as the ones my father and his brothers tell when they have a meal together and set to work embroidering the ever-changing tapestry of their past. There is something both magical and natural about the told story, the wise man spinning a tale at a table in medieval Europe giving way to the mother talking about family history in the kitchen with her children in a small apartment in Chicago. That power of the spoken word was even given a new kind of life at the tail end of the twentieth century, when publishing houses began as a matter of course to do what beforehand only libraries for the blind had done: to release audio versions of books, although audio books sometimes seem to me to have more to do with saving time and alleviating the tedium of travel by car than they do with the need to hear the syllables of a sentence caressed by the human voice.

But the act of reading, the act of seeing a story on the page as opposed to hearing it told—of translating story into specific and immutable language, putting that language down in concrete form with the aid of the arbitrary handful of characters our language offers, of then handing the story on to others in a transactional relationship—that is infinitely more complex, and stranger, too, as though millions of us had felt the need, over the span of centuries, to place messages in bottles, to ameliorate the isolation of each of us, each of us a kind of desert island made less lonely by words. Or, not simply by words, but by words without the evanescence of speech, words that would always be the same, only the reader different each time, so that today, or next year, or a hundred years from now, someone could pick up *A Tale of Two Cities*, turn to the last page, and see that same final sentence, that coda that Dickens first offered readers in 1859: "It is a far, far better thing . . ."

The Sumerians first used the written word to make laundry lists, to keep track of cows and slaves and household goods. But even in such primitive form, the writing down of symbols told of something hugely and richly revolutionary: the notion that one person could have a thought, even if that thought was only about the size of his flocks, and that that thought could be retained and then accessed—rethought, really—by another person in another place and time. The miraculous and transformative quality of this was immediately apparent to some and denied by others: Aristotle turned Alexander the Great into a great reader and champion of books, which led Alexander's successor, Ptolemy I, to create the world's first great library in Alexandria. But Socrates thought books were a waste of time, since they could only "remind one of what one already knows."

Perhaps, seeing his disdain rekindled on the printed page 2500 years after he first felt it—and understanding, surely, that some readers, reading his words, were indeed learning something about Socrates that they had never known before—the great thinker would change his mind. The clay tablet gave way to the scroll and then to the codex, the folded sheets that prefigured the book we hold and sell and treasure today. Wealthy households had books of prayers hand lettered and illuminated by monks; great soldiers kept their dispatches on paper. The French and English modified Gutenberg's press and then mechanized it to set down religious texts and the books of the Bible. Martin Luther nailed his written manifesto against the excesses of the Catholic hierarchy to the door of a church in Wittenberg and began a war of words that led to the Reformation and, eventually, to Protestantism; the Declaration of Independence was set in type and fomented, in relatively few words, a new way for men and women to look at their own government.

And soon publishers had the means, and the will, to publish anything—cookbooks, broadsides, newspapers, novels, poetry, pornography, picture books for children—and to publish them in a form that many people could afford and most could find at the library. Reading became a democratic act, making it possible for the many to teach themselves what the few had once learned from tutors. The president could quote Mark Twain because he had read *The Adventures of Huckleberry Finn*, and the postman could under-

HOW READING CHANGED MY LIFE

stand the reference because he had read it, too. The
Big Lies of demagoguery required more stealth and
cleverness, for careful reading of books and newspapers could reveal their flaws to ordinary people.
Not for nothing did the Nazis light up the night skies
in their cities with the burning of books. Not for
nothing were free white folks in America prohibited
from teaching slaves to read, and slaves in South
Carolina threatened with the loss of the first joint of
their forefingers if they were caught looking at a
book; books became the greatest purveyors of truth,
and the truth shall make you free.

But there was much more than freedom. Reading became the pathway to the world, a world without geographic boundaries or even the steep risers of
time. There was a time machine in our world, but
not the contraption of metal and bolts and motors
imagined even by a man as imaginative as H. G. Wells.
Socrates was wrong: a reader learns what he or she
does not know from books, what has passed and yet
is forever present through print. The mating rituals
of the Trobriand Islanders. The travails of the Don-
ner Party. The beaches at Normandy. The smoke from
the stacks at Auschwitz. Experience, emotion, landscape: the world is as layered as the earth, life cumu-
lative with books. The eyewitnesses die; the written
word lives forever. So does the antipathy that ties two

brothers together in *East of Eden,* and the female search for independent identity in *The Golden Notebook.* How is it that, a full two centuries after Jane Austen finished her manuscript, we come to the world of *Pride and Prejudice* and find ourselves transcending customs, strictures, time, mores, to arrive at a place that educates, amuses, and enthralls us? It is a miracle. We read in bed because reading is halfway between life and dreaming, our own consciousness in someone else's mind. "To completely analyse what we do when we read," wrote E. B. Huey, "would almost be the acme of the psychologist's achievements, for it would be to describe very many of the most intricate workings of the human mind." Yet we take it so for granted, the ability to simply flip the pages and to know what the daughter of a parson, now long dead, once thought of the conventions of matrimony in Regency England, and, certainly, of the relations between men and women into perpetuity.

It is like the rubbing of two sticks together to make a fire, the act of reading, an improbable pedestrian task that leads to heat and light. Perhaps this only becomes clear when one watches a child do it. Dulled to the mystery by years of STOP signs, recipes, form letters, package instructions, suddenly it is self-evident that this is a strange and difficult thing, this making symbols into words, into sentences, into sentiments and scenes and a world imagined in the mind's eye. The children's author Lois Lowry recalled it once: "I remember the feeling of excitement that I had, the first time that I realized each letter had a sound, and the sounds went together to make words; and the words became sentences, and the sentences became stories." The very beginning of a child's reading is even more primal than that, for it is not so much reading but writing, learning to form the letters that make her own name. Naming the world: it is what we do with words from that moment on. All of reading is really only finding ways to name ourselves, and, perhaps, to name the others around us so that they will no longer seem like strangers. Crusoe and Friday. Ishmael and Ahab. Daisy and Gatsby. Pip and Estella. Me. Me. Me. I am not alone. I am surrounded by words that tell me who I am, why I feel what I feel. Or maybe they just help me while away the hours as the rain pounds down on the porch roof, taking me away from the gloom and on to somewhere sunny, somewhere else.

The person who changed my life in this way was named Gertrude LoFurno. She was a friend of my parents, and she owned books. This would seem unremarkable to my children, who have grown up in a house in which virtually every room except for the bathrooms is lined with full shelves. But, growing up, I recall very few houses with books, except for the requisite set of the *Encyclopaedia Britannica* bound in faux leather and conspicuous by their obvious disuse. Although the introduction of mass-market paperbacks at a quarter a copy had forever changed the number of Americans who could afford books, we did not even own very many paperbacks, and I didn't like them much; I liked a book with a certain heft, a kind of solidity of presentation, something heavy as a sack of sugar.

My father had a copy of Machiavelli and a book called *The Art of Worldly Wisdom* by a Jesuit named Balthasar Gracián. I owned an illuminated *Lives of the Saints* and a biography of St. Thérèse of Lisieux, and while I recall a period during which I had a fascination with, even a thirst for bloody martyrdom, it did not last. My mother subscribed to the Reader's Digest Condensed Books, as did the mothers of most of my friends; the magazine began the series in 1950 because of the success of its book section, and the spines of those books, with four titles ranged horizontally, became instantly recognizable to those of us who grew up in the fifties and sixties. They were as middle class at mid-century as the push mower or the cabinet television.

I loved the condensed books, the random nature of the offerings, John Marquand in the same volume with *To Catch a Thief*, Steinbeck paired with *Karen*, the memoir of a child with cerebral palsy written by her mother. I still read the way I learned to read then, savoring the variety of those books: one difficult followed by something fluffier as a reward, one dinner, the other dessert. (Although one condensed book I particularly remember included truncated versions of *The Winter of Our Discontent, The Agony and the Ecstasy,* and *The Making of the President: 1960.*) It would be a stretch to say that those books were particularly literary; there was no Updike, no Mailer or Philip Roth, nothing by John Cheever. But Faulkner was condensed more than once, and Truman Capote, and that unlikely Nobelist, Pearl S. Buck. And the list of titles over nearly fifty years suggests a rich middle-brow vein in American fiction of the fifties and sixties that later ran considerably thinner. There was Herman Wouk's *The Caine Mutiny* and Edna Ferber's *Giant,* Shirley Jackson's *The Haunting of Hill House* and Betty Smith's *A Tree Grows in Brooklyn.*

But most of my books came from the library of the small Catholic private school I attended, which as school libraries went was a good one. The jackets of the books there were ablaze with gold and silver; the librarian always bought whatever book had won the Caldecott and Newbery prizes. Because of this I read some of the best books I had ever read and have ever read since: *A Wrinkle in Time, Charlotte's Web, The Phantom Tollbooth.* But even a good small school library can be fairly quickly exhausted by an indefatigable reader, and once I had read *Island of the Blue Dolphins, The Witch of Blackbird Pond,* and various biographies of Florence Nightingale, Elizabeth I, Joan of Arc, Molly Pitcher—well, I had read them.

I was around ten when Mrs. LoFurno began allowing me to borrow books from her basement, books without plastic covers, without cards in brown paper pockets in the back filled with the names of all the others who had read *Hans Brinker and the Silver Skates* before me. Many of her books were older books, with that particularly sweet dusty smell that old books have; they had bookplates in the front, some of them, sepia colored, vaguely redolent to me of a different sort of world, a world of tea and fires in the fireplace and doilies on chair backs and, in some fashion, a world in which people read, read constantly, avidly, faithfully, in a way in which, in my world, only I did. It was both a world in which, I imagined, books would be treasured, honored, even cosseted on special shelves, and a world that had formed its imaginary self in my mind from books themselves. I cannot recall exactly how I came to believe that Mrs. LoFurno herself had a life lifted almost wholesale from a second-rate Edwardian novel, that she had been raised by aunts after her mother died, a father being a parent, surely, but not one suited for day-to-day meals and such; that she had been sent to convent school of one kind or another. (Actually, it occurs to me now that I may have been confusing her with Sarah Crewe in *A Little Princess*.) There was always a vague whiff of money in my mind about this imagined history, or perhaps it was not money but gentility, a certain sort of Henry Jamesian world that I associated, not only with owning books, but with having whole walls of them. The first time that world actually sprang to life for me was when I was in college and was invited, with the rest of my writing class, to the home of our professor, the literary critic Elizabeth Hardwick. The living room of her New York apartment was two stories high, with books lining the walls. I even remember a library ladder. It was as though my life had somehow come true at the moment I stepped into that room.

Mrs. LoFurno's basement was not so grand, not grand at all, and yet the small spread of books ranged around the room was my first taste of that sort of grandeur. Polyglot, eclectic. In the language of literary criticism, which I have learned to speak, or at least mimic (and, covertly, to despise), it was uneven. There was *Little Women* and lots of Frances Hodgson Burnett and some treacly books for girls written between the world wars. There was A *Girl of the Limberlost*, which no one reads anymore, and there was *Pride and Prejudice*, which everyone should read at least once. The truth is that I cannot recall feeling that there was a great deal of difference between the two. I had no critical judgment at the time; I think children who have critical judgment are as dreadful and unnatural as dogs who wear coats. For some reason I pored over a novel about an adolescent girl entitled *I, Natalie*, which I remember today only as being set in a grim apartment block in Poland and including some suggestion of sex, which was always welcome. There was also *Bonjour Tristesse*, which I found rather flat; I suspect I missed the sense of about half of it, which was true of many books I read at the time.

There was a sense of some torch being exchanged in these trips to the shelves in Mrs. LoFurno's basement, of one reader recognizing another. It did not occur to me until I was much older, an adult myself, that there was anything unusual about doing this with a girl who was not even a relation when Mrs. LoFurno herself had two sons, both around my age, who stayed upstairs while I looked over her books and made my selection. In some covert way, I began to think then of my indefatigable reading fever as a particularly female phenomenon, and perhaps in some fashion to find it as suspect and peculiar as others clearly did.

This sense of women reading, reading, always reading, was in fact reinforced by what I read: Jo March in her attic in *Little Women*, with a book and a bowl of apples; Betsy Ray in the girls' series of the Betsy-Tacy stories, whose friends fulfill their reading requirement for the summer by listening to her tell them all about her beloved *Ivanhoe*; the women of *Gone with the Wind*, sewing and reading aloud while their men were out getting shot. There are very few books in which male characters, much less boys, are portrayed as devoted readers. Actually, there are far fewer coming-of-age books for boys in general, and most are unabashed action stories: raft rides, pirate ships, and battlefields. By contrast, friendship and reading are the central themes of much of the best-loved literature for girls.

When I was younger, I figured that this was because we women had so little to do in the world that the closest we would ever come to real life was to read about it. In fact, that's probably why I loved reading so myself; part of my dissatisfaction with my life was clearly, in retrospect, a dissatisfaction with the traditional roles available to me as a girl at the time, neither of which—nun or housewife, take your pick—particularly suited my temperament.

But it may also be true that the psychology of women lends itself to a keen interest in the vicarious experience of life. I recall, as a columnist, being told by my editor to "talk about what you and your friends are talking about on the telephone." And the truth was that I probably could have gotten a column out of most of my phone calls, determined as we all were to explore, analyze, and understand our own lives through conversation. Perhaps my editor understood intuitively what I came to believe when I considered the abiding interest that so many women have had in reading fiction (and writing it, too): perhaps, as a group, women are more interested in deconstructing the emotional underpinnings of other people's problems, of parsing relationships, connections, and emotions, of living emphatically. Kafka said "a book should serve as the ax for the frozen sea within us." Perhaps we women are more willing to break the ice. Two things that made this possible most often in many of our lives were intimate friendships and reading.

The connection between the two is evident in the invincibility of the book group, that literary coffee klatch which has existed in America for decades but underwent a somewhat surprising resurgence during the last quarter of the twentieth century. It is hard to divine, statistically, who participates and under what circumstances, because there are so many groups in so many places. But the greatest number of book groups seem to be made up of women, and to read very fine books, some of them the same books I found in Mrs. LoFurno's basement. I thought of those book groups one evening at a dinner when a literary critic insisted that book publishing today was "pitched at the interest level of suburban housewives." One collection of suburban housewives in Ohio told me that they had decided to dedicate the fifth year of their book group to Edith Wharton, Jane Austen, and Virginia Woolf; another group, who meet in one another's homes in St. David's on the Main Line of Philadelphia, had chosen during their four years together to read the work of Wallace Stegner, Jane Smiley, and William Styron, among many others, and to devote two consecutive monthly meetings to Tolstoy's *Anna Karenina*. The accepted notion that Americans don't read anymore, or read nothing but junk, was greeted by all of the club's members with disbelief and derision. They personally knew of dozens of book groups: at the local library, at the local bookstore, and at several area churches. Their own had begun on the basis of a list of suggested readings from the daughter of the founding member, who herself had begun a group in New Hampshire. The St. David's women had had to turn potential members away, lest their group grow too big to be collegial, informative, and serious. Each monthly discussion ended with the reading aloud of a short biography of the author and a selection of the reviews the book had received.

"Of course people read," said one of the women. "Every night I read before I went to bed, and I was raising nine kids. I needed to escape, and I needed to use my imagination, and whatever part of my brain was left. It was my greatest pleasure." And, as it had been for me, it was her greatest sense of connection to others, mainly women.

As I grew up enthralled by books, I began to think that women read differently than men. Statistics, although slippery things, suggest some of those differences: a Gallup Poll taken in 1991 showed that women were more likely than men to find reading a more relaxing pastime than watching television. And women are more prolific readers; college-educated women reported reading an average of twenty-five books over the space of a year, while their male counterparts had read only fifteen. Some bookstore owners say their women customers are more likely to read novels, while the men more often choose biographies and history. Perhaps women feel more of a need to escape their own lives and take up those of others than men do.

But it also seemed to me, listening to members of various book clubs ruminate about what they did and why, that, like so much else, women seem to see reading not only as a solitary activity but as an opportunity for emotional connection, not just to the characters in a novel but to those others who are reading or have read the same novel themselves. We pass on beloved books to friends, discuss them on the phone. A collision of two female cultures may have resulted in the sudden glut of book groups in recent years: the women's movement insisted that we do something, be something, use our minds as well as our hearts, while in daily life many of us were still surrounded by the mundane, the sink full of dishes, the car pools, the endless flotsam and jetsam of children. A book group provides one small way for the two selves to coexist: a carefully scheduled occasion for intellectual exercise leavened with female companionship.

And a book provides what it always has: a haven. I remember the first year after my second child was born, what I can remember of it at all, as a year of disarray, of overturned glasses of milk, of toys on the floor, of hours from sunrise to sunset that were horribly busy but filled with what, at the end of the day, seemed like absolutely nothing at all. What saved my sanity were books. What saved my sanity was disappearing, if only for the fifteen minutes before I inevitably began to nod off in bed, into the dark and placid English rooms of Anita Brookner's newest novel, into the convoluted plots of Elmore Leonard's latest thriller, into one of my old favorites, *Breakfast at Tiffany's, Goodbye, Columbus, Our Mutual Friend, Wuthering Heights.* The romantic ramblings of Heathcliff make a piquant counterpoint to dirty diapers, that's for sure. And as it was for me when I was young and surrounded by siblings, as it is today when I am surrounded by children, reading continues to provide an escape from a crowded house into an imaginary room of one's own.

The mere brute pleasure of reading—the sort of
pleasure a cow must have in grazing.
—G. K. CHESTERTON

THE FIRST BOOK that ever seized me so completely by the throat that I read and reread it several times turned out to be one that epitomized both this utter falling into a book that is the hallmark of the way women often read, and the kind of intellectual snobbery that characterizes much of the discussion of books among those people who are considered experts in them. Every reader, I suspect, has a book like this somewhere in his or her past, a book that seemed to hold within it, at that moment, all the secrets of life and love, all the mysteries of the universe. There are other things in life like this as well: the meal perfect in the aspic of memory; the afternoon along the seashore with a breeze and a boat, in hindsight translucent as an opal; a moment of lovemaking. But none of these others can be conjured up exactly as they were. A book—the book that was, for some reason, *the* book—can be reread, unchanged. Only we have changed. And that makes all the difference.

For me that book was a novel written in the early years of the twentieth century. I say a novel, but it is really three novels, or perhaps nine, depending on how you count. But by the time I read it it was called by one name, and known to most readers as one book: *The Forsyte Saga.* Its author, John Galsworthy, won the Nobel Prize for Literature in 1932 on the strength of it, although when undergraduate reading lists are handed out heavy with Fitzgerald and Hemingway there is rarely even a mention of Galsworthy, a man of this century whose work indubitably feels as if it was written in the one before. While the book was a huge success in England in the years between the two world wars, and enjoyed a renaissance when public television networks in America aired a dramatic series based upon it, it has never, to my knowledge, showed up on one of those ever-popular best-book-you-ever-read lists.

Yet for many years I believed it the best book ever written, for no other reason than that I believed in it completely, in the convoluted family relationships, the suffocating Victorian mores, and especially in its characters, particularly Irene, the beautiful and sensitive woman married to the cold, unlovable Soames Forsyte. It is one of those great doorstops of a book that I still approach with delight and then suffer the greatest disappointment if it does not merit the poundage. To me *The Forsyte Saga* was worth every ounce, and every time I came to page 700 my heart would start to sink at the thought of it finishing—and to soar at the thought of starting it again. Even today it is impossible for me to read the final sentence without tears, recognizing in Soames's cri de coeur the universal human yearning of us all: "He might wish and wish and never get it—the beauty and the loving in the world!" To end a novel with an exclamation point— how audacious I found that!

For the purposes of intellectual argument I am prepared here to mount critical opinion against the greatness of *The Forsyte Saga*. I still find it a good read, but no longer a masterwork. In the rereading the book feels less satisfactory than it once did, more plotted than lived, Irene more an idea of a woman than a reality. Perhaps I have read too much since I first read it, at age thirteen—the book was in Mrs. LoFurno's basement, bound in blue cloth—but the triangle between Soames and Irene, Irene and her lover, the architect Philip Bosinney, seems to owe more to *Anna Karenina* than it should, and has less real passion.

But saying this feels like criticizing the face of a

HOW READING CHANGED MY LIFE

lover. The nose may be large, but, oh, the net effect! *The Forsyte Saga* still entrances me; I still find it full of the real roiling emotions of ill-matched marriage and thwarted passion, age and regret and parental love as velvet and thorny as a rose. I own it in a very old edition, the pages of which are loose from their binding, a paperback issued to commemorate the television series, and a well-preserved hardcover edition with an only slightly damaged dust jacket, published by Charles Scribner's Sons. Unlike most books I love, I do not press it upon other readers, even the ones I know best. It would be difficult for me if, for example, my eldest child, my inveterate reader, pronounced it boring or foolish. As for casual acquaintances, I do not care if they read it or not. This is my book.

But I cannot read it without remembering the one-word reaction of the chairman of the English department at my college, when I timidly mentioned it during a discussion of the Great Books, two words which he always said in a way that seemed, ineffably, to emphasize those capital letters. He was talking *Tristram Shandy* at the time; I should have known better. I own perhaps 5000 books today. *Tristram Shandy* is not among them. I do not miss it.

"Galsworthy!" he spit out with a mixture of condescension and disbelief, as though he had found a pit in a fruit that had promised to be seedless. And so a dream died.

(In defense of the professor, he was not alone; V. S. Pritchett wrote a withering assessment of *The Forsyte Saga*, describing it as "the skill of a gentleman amateur on the surface of social life.")

That was how I learned that *The Forsyte Saga* was something I was expected to outgrow, like sucking my thumb, and that it was not likely to be found on any learned reader's list of the so-called Great Books. What books would appear on such a list has become the subject of endless, often tiresome discussions about The Canon (again those capital letters). The discussion took fire, producing much heat, little light, during the last quarter of the twentieth century, when both women and people of color moved from the shadows of some sort of intellectual half-life to a place, more or less, among their male Caucasian peers. Students began to read Ralph Ellison and Anaïs Nin, Colette, and Toni Morrison. As a result there were endless discussions, papers, and books about whether The Canon was being replaced by a polyglot assortment of lesser, more politically correct readings. At an intellectually lively Ivy League university like, say, Columbia, it was possible to start a pitched fight on a walk across campus merely by suggesting that the name "Sappho" should join the names of Plato and Locke on the limestone frieze of Butler Library. The despotism of the educated was in full flower: there was a right way to read, and a wrong way, and the wrong way was worse than wrong—it was middle-brow, that code word for those who valued the enjoyable, the riveting, the moving, and the involving as well as the eternal.

Any reader with common sense was easily lost in this debate, which, among other things, produced critical prose so turgid that anyone who loved the act of reading was easily thrown into confusion, and a blue funk, by it. Besides, most of those so-called middlebrow readers would have readily admitted that the *Iliad* set a standard that could not be matched by *What Makes Sammy Run?* or *Exodus.* But any reader with common sense would also understand intuitively, immediately, that such comparisons are false, that the uses of reading are vast and variegated, and that some of them are not addressed by Homer. Promoters and protectors of The Canon, who were really reeling from the democratization of literature and sudden inclusion of all those women and African-Americans, nevertheless liked to couch this argument in terms of an abandonment of taste of any sort, in both reading and publishing.

As a confirmed Dickensian who had reread *Bleak House* more than I'd read either Dostoyevsky or Stendhal, I was a little puzzled when I arrived at college to discover that there was a kind of covert cloud hanging over the serious discussion of Dickens's work. It took until my senior year to fully apprehend that the great man's great popular success had made him a little suspect, even a century later, in the minds of some literary critics, who clung to the notion that selling well meant pandering, and talent was in inverse proportion to readership.

A look at the best-seller lists of the twentieth century reinforces some of this prejudice: there is plenty of Mickey Spillane and Harold Robbins and those historical novels—*The Silver Chalice, The Robe, The Black Rose*—that were a staple of middle-class home bookshelves. But there is also *Lady Chatterley's Lover, The Great Gatsby,* both *Animal Farm* and *1984, Lolita,* and *The Gulag Archipelago,* none of them what anyone would characterize as beach books.

So what does it mean, that *Peyton Place* by Grace Metalious sold more copies than *Sanctuary* by William Faulkner? It means that reading has as many functions as the human body, and that not all of them are cerebral. One is mere entertainment, the pleasurable whiling away of time; another is more important, not intellectual but serious just the same. "She had learned something comforting," Roald Dahl wrote in *Matilda* of his ever-reading protagonist, "that we are not alone." And if readers use words and stories as much, or more, to lessen human isolation as to expand human knowledge, is that somehow unworthy, invalid, and unimportant?

Discussions about the kind of reading that consti-
tutes a core college curriculum too often ignore
those alternate uses of reading, uses that are quite
apart from educating. Too much of that discussion
concerns itself only with the cerebral and not with
the emotional. Part of the great wonder of reading is
that it has the ability to make human beings feel
more connected to one another, which is a great
good, if not from a pedagogical point of view, at
least from a psychosocial one. When the Center for
the Book at the Library of Congress commissioned
two reporters to travel the country and ask a cross
section of Americans which books had made the
greatest difference in their lives, learning was only a
part of what they got back from their respondents.
One man spoke of the book that helped him over-
come alcoholism, another of a book that helped
comfort him after his mother's death. And more than
a few were like one woman, who said of *The Heart Is
a Lonely Hunter*, "I read it when I was fourteen,
when I didn't feel like anybody understood how I
felt. And here is this book about a fourteen-year-old
girl who had the same feelings I did."

This ability of a book to lessen isolation is important, not simply for personal growth, but for cultural
and societal growth as well. Before the advent of television, books were the primary vehicle for discovering

both the mysteries and the essential human similarities of those a world away. By the fiftieth anniversary of the author's death in the Bergen-Belsen concentration camp, *The Diary of Anne Frank* had sold twenty million copies in fifty-five languages; while its validity as a Holocaust document or a work of art has been debated over and over, there can be no doubt that for several generations of American children who had never heard of the death camps and perhaps never met a Jew, the universality of Anne's adolescent experiences and the horrible specificity of her imprisonment began to open a window on prejudice that might otherwise have longer stayed shut. *The Red Badge of Courage, All Quiet on the Western Front, The Naked and the Dead*: the great novels of war have helped create both patriots and pacifists, among those who have never, will never, see combat. The peculiar jacket copy for *Catcher in the Rye* when it first appeared in paperback, with an awkward representational drawing that predated the now famous austere red jacket, seems to have some sense of its psychological alchemy. "This unusual book," it reads, as though no more specific adjective were available, "may shock you, will make you laugh, and may break your heart—but you will never forget it." And, of course, that is how Salinger's novel has been thought of since it was published in 1951: not in terms of its literary merits, but as a book that has enabled generations of adolescents to feel more like human beings and less like visitors from another planet. Scarcely anyone reads it after age twenty-one, which is irrelevant, perhaps even desirable, to readers under the age of eighteen who find in it proof positive that no one understands them—and that this is a universal condition.

Catcher in the Rye is a signal example of what reading does so well, not only because it has resonated with so many but also because it has enraged so many. When, each year, the American Library Association issues its report on the banning of books by school libraries, it is full of titles about gay life, about sexuality, about witchcraft and the occult. But Salinger's novel is an evergreen on the list, challenged and removed from shelves in virtually every part of the country year after year, even as it continues to be one of the most consistently assigned books on high school reading lists. Parents who have opposed it most frequently complain that it shows a complete disregard for the authority of adults. And indeed it does, which is why adolescents, whose need to disregard the authority of parents is deep and real and transient, perennially place it on their list of favorite books. It challenges the established order, as do many great books—as do many of the books on the banned books list.

My first real encounter with the controversy that can surround a book taught me all this convincingly and on an exceedingly small and intimate scale, taught me about individual taste, about adolescent insurrection, about that great chasm that sometimes arises between one generation and another. My gentle mother was sitting in our living room when she literally hurled the book she had been reading across the coffee table and onto the floor, where chance— and good fortune—made it land not far from my own feet. "This is a dirty book!" my mother said, leaving the room, leaving the book, leaving me to discover that *Portnoy's Complaint* was as funny and intelligent a novel as I had ever read. I have to wonder now, with teenagers in the house, what my mother was thinking that day. Didn't she know that the book felt deeply true at some level, that its sexual content was merely the garment to clothe its important notions about the nature of masculinity? And, above all, didn't she know that I would pick it up and read it the moment she was gone, hearing her distress signal as the clarion cry to forbidden fruit?

It is difficult not to think of that clarion call, of the notion of forbidden fruit, looking at the list of America's banned books. It is difficult not to conclude, too, looking at the list, that the books dominating it are of two sorts: books that are inarguably excellent, and those that merely have the virtue of some sort of truth. The *Banned Books Resource Guide* of 1997 documents efforts to ban Sinclair Lewis,

Moby Dick (because it "conflicts with the values of the community" in a town in Texas), *Of Mice and Men*, and Chaucer. It also has three pages detailing efforts to suppress the young adult novels of Judy Blume, which have sold millions of copies to adolescents who recognized their own problems and pain in their pages. Ms. Blume's *Forever*, about sex between teenagers, was challenged in Scranton because it contains "four-letter words and talked about masturbation, birth control, and disobedience to parents," in Missouri because it promotes "the stranglehold of humanism on life in America," and was moved from the young adult section in Nebraska because it is "pornographic and does not promote the sanctity of . . . family life."

It's an interesting word, that word "pornographic," which, along with the adjective "obscene," has been at the heart of many legal decisions about printed materials. The most entertaining—and telling—exchange was that between Margaret Anderson, the New York bookstore owner who tried to publish *Ulysses* in the United States, and John Quinn, the lawyer who represented her when she was prosecuted for doing so. At the end of the proceedings—lost by the champions of free speech—Quinn warned his client, "And now, for God's sake, don't publish any more obscene literature!"

Anderson replied, "How am I to know when it's obscene?"

"I'm sure I don't know," said the lawyer. "But don't do it."

I repeated that to the eighth grade at the elementary school my three children attend, not far from the store where the intrepid Margaret Anderson sold James Joyce's masterpiece. The librarian there, who knew as much about books for children as many of the industry's best editors, approached Banned Books Week by making a lesson of the banning of books. The eldest students studied the First Amendment. They were remarkably laissez-faire about censorship— the consensus seemed to be that everyone should read everything, which was cheering—but there was general agreement that a book that contained a full frontal nude portrayal of the male form was completely inappropriate for a six-year-old and could be adjudged obscene. I whipped out Maurice Sendak's classic picture book *In the Night Kitchen*, which portrays a small boy named Mickey floating nude, penis and all, through a landscape of enormous flour bags and milk bottles. The eighth grade groaned: *gotcha,* they knew I was saying. But the utter rightness of Mickey's nudity had not been so easily accepted elsewhere; in a school in Missouri shorts had been drawn on the character, and elsewhere the book had been moved from low shelves so only taller, older children could get to it.

As a Catholic girl who grew up in the sixties the

matter of banned books had always fascinated me. Until Vatican II elevated individual conscience to a more central place in the faith, the church kept an Index of Forbidden Books, or Index Librorum Prohibitorum. Balzac was on the list; so were Dumas and Richardson's *Pamela*. Writing of Catholic culture, the psychologist Eugene Kennedy describes an "acceptable" Catholic novel as "generally a pious work that supported and encouraged Catholic ideals and practices and justified the institution and its control over the lives of its adherents. In such works, the good were rewarded, the erring, terribly punished." In my own Catholic home, and at the homes of my relatives, I remember the works of Bishop Fulton J. Sheen, whose radio show was enormously popular, or *The Day Christ Died* by Jim Bishop, a dramatized account of the road to Calvary. (For the more secular audience, there was also *The Day Lincoln Was Shot* by the same author.)

These books were on the bookshelves of many of our homes when I was growing up. By contrast, the dirty books—for it was a simpler, more black-and-white time, when books were not objectionable or titillating, just dirty—were almost universally to be found between the box spring and the mattress of our parents' beds. To read them—and read them we did—we had to make sure that we were alone in the house and that the bedroom door was latched, much as our parents had to do when they were actually engaged in the acts described in the books, which were far less likely to be novels than so-called marriage manuals. (In the case of my own parents, there was a copy of *Tropic of Cancer*, which I think of rather proudly today, being the only evidence I ever saw that they were forward-thinking in matters of literary taste.)

These were the books from which I learned about the mechanics of sex, but of course mechanics was not really what was wanted at all. I learned about sex, among other things, from another Catholic girl, Mary McCarthy, and the enormously popular and controversial roman à clef about her Vassar classmates entitled *The Group*. I have my original paperback copy, published in 1964, its cover softened with a smattering of daisies, and it still falls open, automatically, to the sections in which the reserved Dorothy loses her virginity and then goes to a clinic to buy a birth-control device. Both the description of female orgasm, and of the hot burning embarrassment that a clinic visit can provoke in a newly sexually active woman, remain quite vivid despite several decades and a sexual revolution. I don't know how other young women learned to identify the sensations of climax, or how mortifying a first visit to a gynecologist can be. I know I learned from Mary McCarthy. Come to

think of it, she was my first introduction to lesbianism as well.

But, looking back, I realize it was not so much
the sex as the sedition in the book that I found se-
ductive. Like *Tropic of Cancer*, which I did indeed
filch from my parents' bedroom, or *Portnoy's Complaint*,
or *Peyton Place* or *Lady Chatterley's Lover*, the events of
The Group were matters that I was not supposed to
know about, or even be capable of understanding.
The attention of our elders focused on sexual activity, but perhaps other elements were even more
corrosive of the conventions: disappointment, infi-
delity, duplicity, hypocrisy. In all of those books, too,
there was a sense of forbidden female license that
translated, at some subconscious level, into female
freedom. I can remember my mother poring silently
over a copy of *The Feminine Mystique*, the revolutionary book by Betty Friedan describing the worm at
the core of the fruit of marriage and motherhood.
But I was too young to have either husband or children; I found feminism, my eyes wide at the infinite
variety of the unknown, in *The Group*, in Kay's sui-
cide, Lakey's lesbianism, the sad settling that Dorothy
makes of her life after her one sexual adventure. All
seemed to shout, to belie those daisies on the cover
by shouting, that the lives of intelligent women had to
amount to more than this.

Sedition has been the point of the printed word almost since its inception, certainly since Martin Luther nailed on that church door his list of ninety-five complaints against the established Catholic hierarchy. The printing press led to the Reformation, and to revolutions, political and sexual. Books made atheists of believers, and made believers of millions whose ancestors knew religious texts only as works of art, masterpieces hidden away in the monasteries.

And the opposite was true. Ignorance was the preferred condition of the people by despots. In the essay that begins her book on multiculturalism, a movement toward more inclusionary art and literature which has been both promulgated and ridiculed by books, Hazel Rochman recalls the prevailing ethos of the South African police state that led her and her husband to put their books in a box and bury them in the backyard: "Apartheid has made us bury our books. The Inquisition and the Nazis burned books. Slaves in the United States were forbidden to read books. From Latin America to Eastern Europe and Asia, books have been trashed. But the stories are still there."

For some portion of the human race, political upheaval and reform have come through experience, through the oppression of hereditary monarchs and the corruption of established churches, through seats

at the back of the bus in the Jim Crow South or
sexual harassment in a heretofore all-male assembly
line. But that cannot explain the moral and ethical
awakening of those raised in relative comfort and
ease, never faced with prejudice or denigration. That
was the case with me, and I suspect that it was two
books that began the process of making me a liberal.
One was the Bible, or at least the New Testament, in
which Jesus seemed to take for granted as a necessary
part of existence the need to help those who were
disenfranchised. The other was by Dickens, who
used the gaudy show of character and circumstance
so effectively to communicate the realities of social
injustice. He does it in *Bleak House* with the stranglehold of law, with debtors' prisons in *Little Dorritt*.
But I remember best my first reading of *A Christmas
Carol* in which Scrooge bellows, of those who would
rather die than go to the workhouses, "They had
better do it, and decrease the surplus population."
Visions, not words, change Scrooge's mind, and his
heart, but when he begs the Ghost of Christmas
Present to assure him that his clerk's son, the crippled
Tiny Tim, will not die, the spirit taunts him: "What
then? If he be like to die, he had better do it, and decrease the surplus population.

"Man," adds the Ghost, "if man you be in heart,
not adamant, forbear that wicked cant until you have

discovered What the surplus is, and Where it is." A call to social action, a spiritual invocation, and a climactic moment in a wonderful, and wonderfully well wrought, bit of storytelling—so can a book be personal, political, and entertaining, all at the same time.

Read the greatest stuff but read the stuff that isn't so great, too. Great stuff is very discouraging. If you read only Beckett and Chekhov, you'll go away and only deliver telegrams at Western Union.

—EDWARD ALBEE

IN 1997 KATHERINE Paterson, whose novel *Bridge to Terebithia* has engaged several generations of young people with its story of friendship and loss—and also led to a policy in a school district in Kansas requiring a teacher to list each profanity in required reading and forward the list to parents—gave the Anne Carroll Moore Lecture at the New York Public Library. It was a speech as fine as Ms. Paterson's books, which are fine indeed, and she spoke of the dedication of the children who are her readers: "I increasingly feel a sense of pity toward my fellow writers who spend their lives writing for the speeded-up audience of adults. They look at me, I realize, with a patronizing air, I who only write for the young. But I don't know any of them who have readers who will read their novels over and over again."

As someone who reads the same books over and over again, I think Ms. Paterson is wrong about that, although I know what she means. I have sat on the edge of several beds while *Green Eggs and Ham* was read, or recited more or less from memory; I read *A Wrinkle in Time* three times in a row once, when I was twelve, because I couldn't bear for it to end, wanted them all, Meg and Charles Murry and even the horribly pulsing brain called It, to be alive again as they could only live within my mind, so that I felt as if I killed them when I closed the cover and gave them the kiss of life when my eyes met the words that created their lives. I still reread that way, always have, always will. I suspect there are more of us than Ms. Paterson knows. And I think I know who we are, and how we got that way. We are writers. We danced with the words, as children, in what became familiar patterns. The words became our friends and our companions, and without even saying it aloud, a thought danced with them: *I can do this. This is who I am.*

For some of us, reading begets rereading, and rereading begets writing. (Although there is no doubt which is first, and supreme; as Alberto Manguel writes in his wonderful *A History of Reading*, "I could perhaps live without writing. I don't think I could live without reading.") After a while the story is familiar, the settings known, the characters understood, and there is nothing left to discover but technique. Why that sentence structure and not something simpler, or more complex? Why that way of ordering events instead of something more straightforward, or more experimental? What grabs the reader by the throat? What sags and bags and fails? There are only two ways, really, to become a writer. One is to write. The other is to read. "The rest you learn from books," the novelist B. J. Chute, my senior writing instructor at college, said after she had taught us to send out submissions in a manila envelope, with a SASE for the inevitable rejection. Here is how one of Dickens's friends and his first biographer, John Forster, describes him as a boy: "He was never a first-rate hand at marbles, or peg-top, or prisoners' base; but he had great pleasure in watching the other boys . . . at these games, reading while they played."

I don't know what that boy read as he watched the others, long dead, long dust, play the games he couldn't master, while he began the pas de deux with sentences that would lead to immortality. But I bet it wasn't Shakespeare. Show me a writer who says she was inspired to try by the great masters, and I'll show you someone who is remembering it wrong, or the way she thinks the world wants it remembered. It's too daunting to read *Middlemarch* and say, even to yourself, "I can do that!" Kafka cut his storytelling teeth on Sherlock Holmes, when he was a kid. (Kafka as a kid—now, there's a notion!) And Faulkner's biographer Joseph Blotner writes that young Billy's tastes as a child were lowbrow, a magazine called *The American Boy*: he pored over it, over the short stories that might be comic, sentimental, or uplifting; the articles on famous men; departments such as "The Boy Debater" and "The Boy Coin Collector." Thus was born *The Sound and the Fury*, from riproarers about how the West was won.

That single biographical fact may put to rest one of the other canards of literacy nostalgia, the notion that kids just don't read the way they used to. In his eloquent, impassioned, ultimately alarmist book about reading and technology, *The Gutenberg Elegies,* the critic Sven Birkerts uses a deflating experience teaching undergraduates to argue a "conceptual ledge," a "paradigm shift" in the relations between people and prose. Birkerts's distress stems from his students' lack of interest in what is a challenging story by Henry James, a story of loss and disintegration that resonates with those of us who have begun to experience loss and disintegration. Birkerts admits that as an undergraduate himself he was engaged by writers like Kerouac and Salinger. Yet instead of *A Perfect Day for Bananafish*, he assigns Washington Irving and Henry James and, when his students are not enthusiastic, concludes that technology has interfered with our essential understanding of a complex text. The story reminds me of nothing so much as my elementary school librarian, frowning at the sight of Nancy Drew in our unlined, unscarred hands, or the predictions by our parents that the music of the Beatles and the Rolling Stones meant the end of music as it had heretofore been known.

In fact one of the most pernicious phenomena in assigned reading is the force-feeding of serious work at an age when the reader will feel pushed away, not from the particular book being assigned, but from an entire class of books, or even books in general. So the assigning of *Silas Marner* to high school freshmen is unlikely to make them, later in life, enthusiastic readers of the masterwork *Middlemarch*. At age thirteen, *David Copperfield* often seems less of an invitation to *Bleak House* than a clarion call for Cliffs Notes. (For those who, like me, are determined to raise children with a strong emotional attachment to Dickens, I recommend the reading of *A Christmas Carol* aloud sometime during the holidays.) Perhaps there are indeed children who learned to love books by reading *Moby Dick*, but that sounds like apocryphal remembering to me. Melville could certainly never have made me a writer. My best remembered inspiration, other than a class assignment, which is a source of inspiration to writers mostly overlooked in the rose-colored haze of retelling, was Booth Tarkington's *Seventeen*. That was the book that made me say "I can do that."

Or perhaps it was a combination of two other reading experiences that set me convincingly on the road to becoming a writer. My father had a weakness for humor writing, being a very funny man himself, and I remember how he would laugh over the work of Max Shulman and Jean Shepherd. More than once as a girl I would see him paging through *The Many Loves of Dobie Gillis* or *In God We Trust: All Others Pay Cash* and laughing in the particular way of the human being who is truly tickled, scarcely able to breathe, sometimes seeming to be about to pass out. Another time I remember watching my mother reading a book that she'd loved greatly over the years, *Green Dolphin Street*. It was by Elizabeth Goudge, and was about two sisters in love with the same man. I recall hearing a kind of shuddery sound and turning to see that my mother was weeping. Both these things went deep with me, that words on a page could make my father laugh and my mother cry.

And then finally there are a few sharply remembered moments that are mine alone: Home from school, suspended for bad behavior, I come to the end of *To Kill a Mockingbird* and hear the crack as Jem's arm breaks as clear as I can hear the kitchen clock tick. Lying on the beach listening to a transistor radio, I feel midway through *Main Street* the claustrophobia of small-town life, particularly for women, so acutely that the shiver runs all through me that's said in superstitions to be a ghost walking over my grave.

And one afternoon in college I skip my seminar on writers of the Renaissance so I can finish *Sons and Lovers*, so swept away am I by the passion that a disappointed woman feels for her sons. And I know that I will never, ever write as well as this, but that if anything even dimly like this power, to enthrall, to move, to light up the darkness of daily life, lies hidden like a wartime cryptogram within the Royal manual typewriter on my dorm room desk, I must try to make a go of it. Why would anyone aspire to be president of the United States or of General Motors if they could write like D. H. Lawrence instead? That's what I remember thinking.

That's not to say that I immediately set myself the work of constant writing; that, too, is a writer's life story that I suspect. But I did begin to think of myself as a writer, although I was not sure what sort of writer I was. Like most young people, I went through a romance with poetry, enamored of the music and the rhythm of the words, and by the soothing notion that there need be so much less to the product than there was in even a slender novel. In my own life, this

romance fell in a predictable period. It came after the
end of elementary school, when poetry was something between a punishment and a spelling bee, "The
Children's Hour" committed to memory, and college,
when I took a modern poetry course from the same
professor who found Galsworthy beneath notice. He
had a fine, sonorous voice that rang in the small stuffy
classroom, vying successfully with the sound of traf-
fic on Broadway, and those half glasses that I still as-
sociate with intelligence even though I now wear,
and loathe, them. And when he read Ezra Pound's
"Hugh Selwyn Mauberley" aloud, dipping his out-
sized shaggy head to the page—"For three years, out
of key with his time/He strove to resuscitate the dead
art/Of poetry; to maintain 'The Sublime'/In the old
sense. Wrong from the start"—I knew that, whatever
else I might be, I was no poet. My books from that
course are full of painstaking marginalia, as though if
I paid close enough attention the bird would fly in
my breast. But I didn't have poetry in me. I wrote fiction in college, and then for many years I wrote fact,
as best I could gather, discern, and describe it, as a
newspaper reporter. Then I wrote fiction again. Reading taught me how to do it all.

"Books are over," the editor of a journal to be
found only on the Internet told me one day at a con-
ference on the future of the newspaper business. Just
my luck. After all these years of reading books I'd fi-

nally written one; when I took time to alphabetize my shelves, it came between Proust and Ayn Rand, which seemed representative of how I'd read all my life, between the great and the merely engagingly popular. I could still remember the time I had held my first hardcover book. The Federal Express truck raised a cloud of gravel and dust on a country road as I ripped into the envelope, removed the book, and lifted it up and down in my outstretched hands, just to feel the heft of it, as though it was to be valued by weight. I held it the way I'd seen babies held at religious ceremonies, a bris, perhaps, or a baptism. Hardcovers: every writer's ultimate ambition, whether she admits it or not.

It was a fearsome frisson that ripped through the business, the business of writing, the business of publishing, the business of newspapering, when I was well into all three. The computer had become like the most miraculous sort of technological Swiss Army knife: each time you thought you knew what it could do, it turned out that it could do more, faster, better, more accurately. I wrote my first novel on a big clunker of a machine that wheezed slightly when it stored information and had a mere 256 kilobits of memory. It just managed to hold the book, the word-processing program, and a few other odds and ends. My third novel was composed on a machine that fits into my handbag and weighs slightly more than a premature baby. The program corrects my punctuation and capitalization as I type; when I try to type a stand-alone lowercase *I*, it inflates it into a capital letter, correcting me peremptorily, certain I've made a mistake. I could keep a dozen copies of my book on its hard disk and it wouldn't even breathe hard.

And there was less than a decade between the publication of those two books.

So it became easy, as the age of the computer washed in a wave of modems and cybersurfers over the United States at the end of the twentieth century, to believe those who said that books need never leave the soul of this new machine at all, that the wave of the future was this: *The Age of Innocence* on-line, to be called up and read with the push of a VIEW button; *The Fountainhead* via the Internet, perhaps with all the tiresome objectivist polemical speeches set in a different font for easy skipping-over (or even the outright deletions that Ayn Rand's editor should have taken care of). No paper, no shelf space, and the ultimate democratization of reading: a library in a box much smaller than a single volume of the old leather-bound *Encyclopaedia Britannica*. To all the old fears—of lack of literacy, of interest, of quality—was added the fear of microchips.

A small skirmish in these technowars broke out in the summer of 1997 in the pages of *The Horn Book*, the journal of children's literature, and it was representative of both the worst-case scenarios and the realities of the future of publishing in an era of tear-away technology. A writer and librarian named Sarah Ellis tried an experiment: she read on a laptop computer a book for children called *The End of the Rainbow*. But this was not just any book: it exemplified the greatest fears of those who love children's literature, and know how difficult it can be to publish in a cost-conscious age. *The End of the Rainbow* was part of a series of Danish books about a boy named Buster published by Dutton; the sales trajectory of its predecessors had convinced the publisher to offer it free on the Internet rather than go to the expense of publishing it in book form.

Ms. Ellis gave Buster on the computer a fair shake, but she found the experience ultimately unsatisfactory. She concluded that the process of scrolling down, reading in a linear fashion, on a machine she associates with haste, were all antithetical to reading for pleasure. "The screen," she says, "turned me into a reluctant reader." When she went to the library and took out an earlier bound Buster book, her reluctance disappeared. "I experienced that feeling of surrender, of putting myself in someone's hands, which is one of the great pleasures of fiction," she wrote. And she reclaimed the experience of a book, pure and simple: "the soft scrape of my fingers against the pages, the glissando sound of flipping back to a previous chapter." The scrolling of the screen had not been the equivalent of turning the pages. A laptop is portable, but not companionable.

Ms. Ellis believed her experiment raised many questions about the future of reading in the face of the ascendancy of computers, questions that will be raised over and over again in the years to come. But, reading her words, I found more questions answered than asked, and one essential one settled to my satisfaction. At the time that technocrats had predicted the imminent death of the book as we knew it, all of us in the world of print were in a kind of frenzy about how new technology would change our old businesses. In the five years between my first job as a copy girl and my hiring at *The New York Times* as a reporter, big papers had begun to retire their typewriters and bring in computer systems on which reporters would produce the day's copy and editors edit it. It was a modest revolution, given the advances still to come, but a revolution not without pain; one of the *Times's* most venerable reporters insisted he was too old to learn new tricks, and his copy had to be transcribed into the computer from the copy paper he continued to use in his old manual typewriter.

But the real revolution was said to be coming in the product itself. Panel after panel was held at journalism conventions about whether newspapers would be replaced by the downloading of the day's news onto a computer screen. It seemed only sensible to those whose correspondence had become characters sent by modem from one computer to another instead of a file of business letters, inevitable that the collection of folded newsprint that landed on the doormat with a *thwap* before daybreak each morning could simply be replaced by a virtual newspaper in a computer in the kitchen, coffee cup beside the keyboard.

Perhaps that may someday come to pass, in one form or another; perhaps someday it will seem quaint that anyone ever doubted that the printed book between hard or soft covers was in its twilight at the end of the twentieth century. But the decade after the initial panic over the demise of printing upon paper seemed to foreshadow a very different end. News indeed appeared on computers; so did magazines, some created expressly for on-line users. There were even books like the Buster book that Dutton put on the Internet rather than risk commercial failure. But none of them convincingly supplanted the more conventional product. Both those in the business of books and those in the business of computer technology realized something that we readers apprehended most deeply in our hearts: that people are attached, not only to what is inside books, but to the object itself, the old familiar form that first took shape four centuries ago. A laptop computer is a wondrous thing; it is inconceivable to me now that I ever did without one, particularly in writing and revision. (There are still, of course, those novelists who like to speak fervently of writing by hand in special lined journals, or using the old Royal typewriter they were given when they went away to Choate forty years before. Not me.) But a computer is no substitute for a book. No one wants to take a computer to bed at the end of a long day, to read a chapter or two before dropping off to sleep. No one wants to take one out of a purse on the New York City subway to pass the time between Ninety-sixth Street and the World Trade Center. No one wants to pass *Heidi* on disk down to their daughter on the occasion of her eighth birthday, or annotate William Carlos Williams on-screen. At least, no one wants to do it *yet*, even those who are much farther along the cybercurve than I am. The dis-ease Ms. Ellis felt reading a book on the computer, which she described so eloquently in her *Horn Book* article, is what so many of the rest of us feel, and why the book continues to prosper. Ms. Ellis wonders if this is generational, if she finds reading a screen less satisfactory than do children born to its blandishments. But I have three of those children, and while they play games, trade mail, and do plenty of research on their computers, they do most of their reading in plain old ordinary books, some that belonged to me years ago. They seem to like it that way. My youngest grew up with a copy of *Arthur's Teacher Trouble* on

CD-ROM, an interactive version of the picture book that allowed her to use her mouse to make desks open and birds fly. But she never gave up reading the version on paper. "I like the real book," she said.

And a real book, not a virtual version, is more often than not what's wanted. After all, the publisher of Dutton Children's Books did not decide to publish *The End of the Rainbow* on-line because children were clamoring to read it on the computer. His reasons were financial, not philosophical; he simply did not believe he could afford the loss that the book would incur in conventional publication. The prophets of doom and gloom and the virtual library may use this to generalize about a future in which hundreds, perhaps thousands of wonderful books are never published at all. But the fact is that publishing in all its incarnations—small presses, large presses, vanity presses, university presses—produces many more new titles today than it did fifty or a hundred years ago. More than 350,000 new books were added to the Library of Congress in 1995 alone; that institution, founded with funding of $5000 two centuries ago, now has 200 times the number of items once found in the legendary library in Alexandria.

And if some new books only manage to make their way onto the Internet, isn't that better than losing them entirely? New technology offered the publisher of Dutton Children's Books, Christopher

Franceschelli, some useful middle ground between taking a substantial financial loss and not offering the book to readers at all. He wrote eloquently in a letter to *The Horn Book*, "We live in an era of transition perhaps not all that dissimilar to that of five hundred years ago. Then an entire culture had to wrestle with the meaning of the Western re-invention of movable type. Even then there were those who bemoaned the loss of texture, when the individually crafted, individually illuminated manuscript, with rubricated initials and tooled leather bindings, gave way to the radically simple black and white pages mechanically produced by Gutenberg and his descendants. Indeed there are those who would argue that the entire Protestant movement was only possible once the Book had lost its totemic value as literal manifestation of the divine Word to reappear as the book— cheap, portable, with a mutable text accessible to (and interpretable by) one and all."

And in his history of reading, Albert Manguel concludes, "It is interesting to note how often a technological development—such as Gutenberg's— promotes rather than eliminates that which it is supposed to supersede." Consider, for instance, the thousands of books sold every day on-line. In at least one way, those computer services that were said to spell *finis* to book buying in America have instead succeeded in making it easier for the technologically adept.

Katherine Paterson, in her library speech, took the long view, too, describing her despair at trying to find information on an on-line service and turning to an old encyclopedia and finding it there instead, but noting, too, "I think it well behooves us to realize that we are not the first generation to fear the changes that seem to engulf us. Plato, lest we forget, argued in the *Dialogues* that if people learned to read and write, poetry would disappear, for it was only in the oral tradition that poetry could be preserved properly."

Well, Plato was wrong. And so, I believe, are those people predicting the demise of the book, particularly its death by microchip. The discussions surrounding the issue always remind me of the discussions from my childhood about the gastronomic leap forward occasioned by the development of astronaut food. Soon, we heard, we would be able to eat an entire Sunday dinner in the form of a pill. Soon a Creamsicle could be carried around in your pocket, run under the hose, and reconstituted on a warm day, almost as good as new.

It's thirty years since man first walked on the moon, and when people sit down to a big old-fashioned supper it is still a plate of roast beef and mashed potatoes, not a capsule and a glass of water. When they buy a Creamsicle, it's three-dimensional, wet and cold and wonderful. That's because people like the thing itself. They don't eat mashed potatoes with gravy because they just need to be nourished, but because mashed potatoes and gravy are wonderful in so many ways: the heat, the texture, the silky slide of the gravy over your tongue. And that is the way it is with books. It is not simply that we need information, but that we want to savor it, carry it with us, feel the heft of it under our arm. We like the thing itself.

It is not possible that the book is over. Too many people love it so. It is possible that it has fallen upon hard times, but finding the evidence to prove this is more challenging than many people may think. It is true that there are almost no serializations of books in magazines anymore, a form of book that once made novels accessible for millions of readers who could not afford hardcovers. It is true that department stores no longer sell books, and that many of what pass for bookstores seem closer to gift shops, with far too many datebooks and trinkets. It's a little terrifying, the fact that in many of the mall stores there is an entire long wall classified as Fiction and a small narrow section to one side of it called Literature. That second, smaller, section is reserved largely for dead people, dead people who represent much of the best the world of words has had to offer over its long span.

But the ultimate truth is that they aren't dead, those people. The writers of books do not truly die; their characters, even the ones who throw themselves in front of trains or are killed in battle, come back to life over and over again. Books are the means to immortality: Plato lives forever, as do Dickens, and Dr. Seuss, Soames Forsyte, Jo March, Scrooge, Anna Karenina, and Vronsky. Over and over again Heathcliff wanders the moor searching for his Cathy. Over and over again Ahab fights the whale. Through them all we experience other times, other places, other lives. We manage to become much more than our own selves. The only dead are those who grow sere and shriveled within, unable to step outside their own lives and into those of others. Ignorance is death. A closed mind is a catafalque.

I still remember sitting in the fading afternoon one day in a rambling old house in the country speaking to the elderly matriarch of one of America's great publishing families, a woman known for her interest in all things political, social, intellectual. Near the end of our conversation she squared her shoulders, looked sharply into some middle distance behind me, and said, as though to herself, "I can't read any longer." The words were sad and sonorous as a church bell, and I felt that she had pronounced a sort of epitaph upon herself, and I felt that she felt it too: I can't read any longer.

Yet in her sorrow there was joy, the remembered joy of someone who had been a reader all her life, whose world had been immeasurably enlarged by the words of others. Perhaps it is true that at base we readers are dissatisfied people, yearning to be elsewhere, to live vicariously through words in a way we cannot live directly through life. Perhaps we are the world's great nomads, if only in our minds. I travel today in the way I once dreamed of traveling as a child. And the irony is that I don't care for it very much. I am the sort of person who prefers to stay at home, surrounded by family, friends, familiarity, books. This is what I like about traveling: the time on airplanes spent reading, solitary, happy. It turns out that when my younger self thought of taking wing, she wanted only to let her spirit soar. Books are the plane, and the train, and the road. They are the destination, and the journey. They are home.

READING LISTS ARE arbitrary and capricious, but most people like them, and so do I. My most satisfying secondhand experiences as a reader have come through recommending books, especially to my children. And I will never forget the summer reading lists I created for my sister when she lived with us during college vacations. One day she came in with a worn paperback copy of *Pride and Prejudice* and said peevishly, "Just tell me now if she marries Mr. Darcy, because if she doesn't I'm not finishing the book." How pleased Jane Austen would have been. How pleased I was.

Here are a few arbitrary and capricious suggestions for fellow readers:

10 Big Thick Wonderful Books That Could Take You a Whole Summer to Read (but Aren't Beach Books)

Gone with the Wind by Margaret Mitchell
Vanity Fair by William Makepeace Thackeray
East of Eden by John Steinbeck
The Forsyte Saga by John Galsworthy
Buddenbrooks by Thomas Mann
Can You Forgive Her? by Anthony Trollope
Sophie's Choice by William Styron
Henry and Clara by Thomas Mallon
Underworld by Don DeLillo
Lonesome Dove by Larry McMurtry

10 Nonfiction Books That Help Us Understand the World

The Decline and Fall of the Roman Empire
by Edward Gibbon
The Best and the Brightest by David Halberstam
Lenin's Tomb by David Remnick
Lincoln by David Herbert Donald
Silent Spring by Rachel Carson
In Cold Blood by Truman Capote
How We Die by Sherwin Nuland
The Unredeemed Captive by John Demos
The Second Sex by Simone de Beauvoir
The Power Broker by Robert A. Caro

10 Books That Will Help a Teenager Feel More Human

The Catcher in the Rye by J. D. Salinger
A Separate Peace by John Knowles
Lost in Place by Mark Salzman
What's Eating Gilbert Grape? by Peter Hedges
The World According to Garp by John Irving
Bloodbrothers by Richard Price
A Tree Grows in Brooklyn by Betty Smith
To Kill a Mockingbird by Harper Lee
The Heart Is a Lonely Hunter by Carson McCullers
The Member of the Wedding by Carson McCullers

The 10 Books I Would Save in a Fire
(If I Could Save Only 10)

Pride and Prejudice by Jane Austen
Bleak House by Charles Dickens
Anna Karenina by Leo Tolstoy
The Sound and the Fury by William Faulkner
The Golden Notebook by Doris Lessing
Middlemarch by George Eliot
Sons and Lovers by D. H. Lawrence
The Collected Poems of W. B. Yeats
The Collected Plays of William Shakespeare
The House of Mirth by Edith Wharton

10 Books for a Girl Who Is Full of Beans (or Ought to Be)

Little Women by Louisa May Alcott
Julius: The Baby of the World by Kevin Henkes
Betsy in Spite of Herself by Maud Hart Lovelace
Anne of Green Gables by Lucy Maud Montgomery
The Diary of a Young Girl by Anne Frank
The BFG by Roald Dahl
A Wrinkle in Time by Madeline L'Engle
Madeline by Ludwig Bemelmans
Catherine, Called Birdy by Karen Cushman
The True Confessions of Charlotte Doyle
by Avi, Ruth E. Murray

10 Mystery Novels I'd Most Like to Find in a Summer Rental

An Unsuitable Job for a Woman by P. D. James
Gaudy Night by Dorothy Sayers
The Beekeeper's Apprentice by Laurie P. King
Rebecca by Daphne du Maurier
Get Shorty by Elmore Leonard
Dancers in Mourning by Margery Allingham
The Way Through the Woods by Colin Dexter
The Adventures of Sherlock Holmes
by Arthur Conan Doyle
Brat Farrar by Josephine Tey
The Spy Who Came in from the Cold
by John Le Carré

10 Books Recommended by a Really Good Elementary School Librarian

The View from Saturday by E. L. Konigsburg
Frindle by Andrew Clements
My Daniel by Pam Conrad
The Houdini Box by Brian Selznick
Good Night, Mr. Tom by Michelle Magorian
No Flying in the House by Betty Brock
My Father's Dragon by Ruth Stiles Gannett
Habibi by Naomi Shihab Nye
Mudpies: And Other Recipes: A Cookbook for Dolls
by Marjorie Winslow
The Story of May by Mordecai Gerstein

10 Good Book-Club Selections

Fraud by Anita Brookner
Charming Billy by Alice McDermott
The Book of Ruth by Jane Hamilton
The Rise of Silas Lapham
by William Dean Howells
The Stone Diaries by Carol Shields
Mrs. Dalloway by Virginia Woolf
The Patron Saint of Liars by Ann Patchett
Sister Carrie by Theodore Dreiser
Paris Trout by Pete Dexter
Eden Close by Anita Shreve

10 Modern Novels That Made Me Proud to Be a Writer

The Sweet Hereafter by Russell Banks
White Noise by Don DeLillo
Martin Dressler by Steven Millhauser
True Confessions by John Gregory Dunne
The Death of the Heart by Elizabeth Bowen
The French Lieutenant's Woman by John Fowles
Falconer by John Cheever
The Bluest Eye by Toni Morrison
The Information by Martin Amis
Portnoy's Complaint by Philip Roth

10 of the Books My Exceptionally Well Read Friend Ben Says He's Taken the Most From

Herzog by Saul Bellow
Coming Up for Air by George Orwell
Something of an Achievement by Gwyn Griffin
Lucky Jim by Kingsley Amis
The Collected Poems of William Butler Yeats
Walden by Henry David Thoreau
The Moon and Sixpence by Somerset Maugham
Riders of the Purple Sage by Zane Grey
Heretics by G. K. Chesterton
The Wapshot Chronicles by John Cheever

(With addendum: "Now I can't believe I settled for that list. What about William Maxwell's *The Folded Leaf*, or Elizabeth Bowen's *The House in Paris?*")

10 Books I Just Love to Read, and Always Will

Main Street by Sinclair Lewis
My Ántonia by Willa Cather
The Lion, the Witch, and the Wardrobe
by C. S. Lewis
Wuthering Heights by Emily Brontë
Jane Eyre by Charlotte Brontë
The Group by Mary McCarthy
The Blue Swallows by Howard Nemerov (poetry)
The Phantom Tollbooth by Norton Juster
A Christmas Carol by Charles Dickens
Scoop by Evelyn Waugh

Acknowledgments

M OST OF THE books used as source material are acknowledged within the body of this extended essay. But I would like to especially thank Alberto Manguel for his marvelous *A History of Reading*. Edward de Grazia's *Girls Lean Back Everywhere* provides an invaluable education on the issues of literary censorship. I'm also grateful for two reference books, *Writing Changes Everything,* edited by Deborah Brodie, and *The Columbia Book of Quotations*, edited by Robert Andrews.

Many dedicated readers helped me think about the issues raised in this book. I would like to thank Eden Ross Lipson, Eugene Kennedy, Una Cadegan,

Eden Stewart Eisman at St. Luke's School in New York City, Carol Miles at the American Booksellers Association, Joyce Meskis of the Tattered Cover bookstore in Denver, and the members of the St. David's book club, who invited me in for coffee and conversation one winter night: M. Karen Redmond, Maud Walker, Joyce Guyer, Sylvia Severance, Patricia Graham, Jeanne McGuigan, Diane O'Hara, Jean Welz, Ann Crapo, Linda Edie, Margaret Murphy, Phyllis Hughes.

As always, Kate Medina and Amanda Urban make everything possible for me professionally. And personally there are Janet Maslin and Ben Cheever, Quin, Christopher, Maria, and Gerry Krovatin.

A special thank-you to teachers and librarians. If not you, not me.

ABOUT THE AUTHOR

ANNA QUINDLEN is the author of the national bestseller, *A Short Guide to a Happy Life,* and three bestselling novels. Her *New York Times* column "Public and Private" won a Pulitzer Prize in 1992, and a selection of these columns was published as *Thinking Out Loud.* She is also the author of a collection of her "Life in the 30's" columns, *Living Out Loud,* and two children's books, *The Tree That Came to Stay* and *Happily Ever After.* She is currently a columnist for *Newsweek* and lives with her husband and children in New York City.